DOGS

by Nancy Furstinger

Content Consultant
Alexandra Protopopova, MS, ABD
Psychology Department
University of Florida

CORE
LIBRARY

Published by ABDO Publishing Company, PO Box 398166, Minneapolis, MN 55439. Copyright © 2014 by Abdo Consulting Group, Inc. International copyrights reserved in all countries. No part of this book may be reproduced in any form without written permission from the publisher. The Core Library™ is a trademark and logo of ABDO Publishing Company.

Printed in the United States of America,
North Mankato, Minnesota
092013
012014

♻ THIS BOOK CONTAINS AT LEAST 10% RECYCLED MATERIALS.

Editor: Mirella Miller
Series Designer: Becky Daum

Library of Congress Cataloging-in-Publication Data
Furstinger, Nancy.
  Dogs / by Nancy Furstinger.
      pages cm. -- (The smartest animals)
  Includes bibliographical references and index.
  ISBN 978-1-62403-165-6
  1. Dogs--Juvenile literature. 2. Animal intelligence--Juvenile literature. I. Title.
  SF426.5.F87 2014
  636.7--dc23
                        2013027283

Photo Credits: Shutterstock Images, cover, 1, 14, 17, 20, 28, 30, 45; Tatiana Gass/Shutterstock Images, 4; Ryan Miller/Invision/AP Images, 6; iStockphoto/Thinkstock, 7, 9, 11, 22; Michal Ninger/Shutterstock Images, 7 (far right); Digital Vision/Thinkstock, 12; Jupiterimages, 18, 43; Fuse/Thinkstock, 25, 26; North Wind/North Wind Picture Archives, 32; Red Line Editorial, 34; Manuel Balce Ceneta/AP Images, 36; Mike Lawrence/The Gleaner/AP Images, 39; Kelly Nelson/Shutterstock Images, 40

CONTENTS

CHAPTER ONE

DIFFERENT DOGS

A black Labrador retriever named Soot bursts with energy. Soot's human companion, Lorrie, thought Soot would make a good search and rescue dog. Lorrie and Soot started to go to search and rescue classes together. Soot learned how to pick up human scents in the air. This would help him find missing people in the future.

Many households around the world have a dog as a pet. These super-smart animals are also loving companions.

Actress Megyn Price meets 2012 Search and Rescue winner, Soot.

Soot got to practice his skills when an elderly hunter went missing on November 30, 2011. Soot sniffed a coat the hunter had left behind. Then Soot picked up the scent and led the search team five miles (8 km) away to a mountaintop. Soot and the team searched overnight until they found the hunter alive at 5:30 a.m. Soot had sniffed out the hunter! Soot received his favorite reward, a green tennis ball, for

Size Comparison Chart
Dogs range in size from small to extra large. In between are hundreds of breeds. This chart compares dogs of various sizes. Look at the chart, and think about how these different dogs compare to each other. Then write sentences comparing big and little dogs.

saving the hunter's life. Soot was the 2012 American Humane Association Hero Dog Award winner.

An Amazing Assortment

Dog breeds come in a variety of sizes and shapes. They range from the tiny Chihuahua, which weighs less than 6 pounds (3 kg), to the giant English mastiff, which can weigh up to 343 pounds (156 kg). The American Kennel Club recognizes more than 400 different dog breeds around the world.

All dog breeds descend directly from the gray wolf. Approximately 15,000 years ago, dogs started living around humans. Eventually humans began to handle and interact with dogs. Dogs have been companions of humans ever since.

Humans breed dogs for different purposes. The American Kennel Club divides breeds into seven groups. The first group is sporting dogs, such as Labrador retrievers. Sporting dogs locate and bring back game in the water and the woods. Hounds are the second group of dogs. Beagles are one breed in this group. They use their sharp sense of smell and their energy to chase other animals. The third group is terriers, such as the Airedale terrier. These dogs are active hunters and expert diggers.

Marvelous Mixes

One of the most common dogs in the world is a combination of breeds. This is called a mixed-breed dog. In the past, a mixed-breed dog's family tree was a guessing game. Now a DNA test of a dog can reveal the combination of breeds in its family history.

Alaskan malamute and Siberian husky dogs are part of the working breed of dogs. They are very good at sled racing.

A fourth group includes herding dogs, such as collies, which guard livestock. Working breeds are included in a fifth group. Alaskan malamutes, one dog breed in this group, perform a variety of jobs, such as pulling sleds and guarding property. Nonsporting breeds, such as dalmatians, make up the sixth group. This group was bred for different purposes, such as performing in circuses. The final group is the toy breeds. The Pekingese is meant for sitting on laps.

Super Senses

All dogs share super senses. Dogs explore the world using their top sense: smell. While humans rely mostly on sight, dogs rely on smell. A dog's sense of smell is anywhere from 10,000 to 100,000 times more powerful than a human's sense of smell. This means dogs can smell odors so faint a human would never smell them. A dog can smell if one teaspoon of sugar has been added to a cup of coffee.

A dog's hearing is also better than a human's hearing abilities. Dogs can hear sounds that are four times the distance humans can hear. Dogs can move

Canine Detectives

Bloodhounds are famous for their amazing noses. These hounds create an odor image when they sniff a scent. The odor image helps the bloodhound see its surroundings through smells. Then they are able to follow a scent trail until they discover the source of the scent. If police officers are trying to track down a criminal, a bloodhound's nose will track the person down. The bloodhound's nose is so sharp that evidence found by this dog is accepted in a court of law.

Chihuahuas' upright ears help them hear sounds from a great distance.

their 18 ear muscles in the direction of sounds. This helps them hear a sound better. Dogs with upright ears, like the Chihuahua, have an advantage over dogs whose ears hang down, like the Labrador retriever.

A dog's sense of sight is not as strong as its other senses. Dogs cannot detect all colors. They see shades of blue, gray, and yellow. However, dogs can see better than humans in dim light.

Dogs can taste foods that are sweet, sour, bitter, and salty. Their sense of taste is not as advanced as humans'. This is why dogs gulp down their food

Taste is one sense that is not as advanced for dogs.

without seeming to taste it. Dogs' senses of taste and smell are linked. This is why they sniff out the stinky treats and gobble them up.

Dogs can sense hot, cold, pain, and pressure through nerve endings, just like humans. These nerve endings are everywhere on their bodies. Dogs also rely on their whiskers for the sense of touch. Whiskers above the eyes, below the jaw, and on the nose help dogs navigate places.

Scientist Alexandra Horowitz writes about what dogs see and smell in her book. Here she paints a picture of the dog experience:

> *We naturally imagine that dogs are more or less like us— only less sophisticated, less smart, with less going on in their heads. This is simply wrong. When we realize what they can sense that we cannot, a new picture appears: one in which the dog is in an extraordinarily rich sensory world, with complex social interactions, and with a special ability to read our behavior. Dogs don't see the world like we do: they "see" mostly through smell. . . . Their vision is pretty good, not as finely detailed and colored as ours is, but it is secondary to their ability to see the world through their noses. Even imagining that is difficult for us vision-centered folks.*

> *Source: Alexandra Horowitz. "Author Interview." Simon & Schuster. Simon & Schuster, n.d. Web. Accessed August 2, 2013.*

What's the Big Idea?

Take a close look at Horowitz's words. What is her main point about dogs' senses? What evidence is used to support her ideas? Come up with a few sentences showing how Horowitz uses two or three pieces of evidence to support her main point.

CHAPTER TWO

DOG YEARS

Female dogs are pregnant for approximately nine weeks. The number of puppies born depends on a dog's size. Toy breeds rarely have more than two puppies. Small breeds usually have one to four puppies. Medium breeds have an average of four to eight puppies. Large breeds can give birth to up to 10 to 12 puppies. Female dogs will generally mate

Puppies need love and attention from their mothers in the first few weeks of their lives.

with multiple males throughout their lives. Some females only have puppies once, though.

Puppy Personality

The first eight weeks of a dog's life form its personality. During this stage, the puppy socializes with its mother and siblings. The puppy is also exposed to many different things, such as humans or toys. The more things the puppy experiences, the less fearful it will be as an adult. Puppies playfully wrestle and bite each other to better understand how to relate to one another. As the puppies play, they learn important lessons about how to behave. The self-confident puppy learns to think and solve problems. Puppies can go home with families at eight weeks old.

Puppies are born completely helpless. They are unable to see or hear. At this stage, the mother dog is the center of their world. She will feed her toothless puppies and then help them get rid of waste. Her puppies will crawl forward and whine when they need her.

Puppies spend all their time sleeping, nursing, and growing. After about two weeks, their eyes and ears open and their teeth come in. They learn how to balance

By four weeks old, puppies can walk and wrestle with their brothers and sisters.

on four legs and wag their tails. Their bodies and brains both grow rapidly.

Puppies mature faster than humans. Dogs are considered teenagers by the time they are between 6 and 18 months old. Smaller breeds grow faster than larger breeds and live longer. The biggest breeds are considered elderly at the age of six.

Unlike household dogs, wolves form family packs to live in.

Leader of the Pack

Wolves form family packs that include between five and nine members. An alpha male and alpha female lead the pack. This top pair of wolves is the father and mother of the pack. They are also the only breeding couple. Their puppies make up part of the pack, along with some nonrelated wolves.

Household dogs are not born into packs. The mother dog trains her puppies how to behave. She corrects them when they are naughty and rewards them when they are obedient.

Psychologist Stanley Coren is known for his series of nonfiction dog books. Here he shares an interesting story about how dogs think:

> 'Come on, Shadow, sit down!' the boy commanded. The dog shuffled its feet uncertainly as the boy complained, 'See, he just doesn't know what he's supposed to do.' Then the dog did a very odd thing: he lowered himself to a sitting position with his chest low and forward, and then, with his rear end still on the ground, he began to drag himself toward the boy. . . . It dawned on the instructor what was going on: The boy's communication was so imprecise that he had actually given Shadow three conflicting commands, effectively telling the dog to come, to sit, and to lie down. The hard-working and very intelligent animal had then desperately tried to perform all three actions at once, resulting in his bizarre behavior.

> Source: Stanley Coren. *The Intelligence of Dogs. New York: The Free Press*, 2005. Print. 257.

Back It Up

In this passage, Coren is using evidence to support a point. Write a paragraph describing the point Coren is making. Then write down two or three pieces of evidence Coren uses to make the point.

CHAPTER THREE

CLEVER CANINES

Scientists believe dogs study human behavior to solve problems. Some dogs might figure out how to open a sliding door through trial and error. They experiment with different methods until they find one that works. Other dogs have worked out a smarter solution. They watch humans and then copy how to open the door.

Dogs are more intelligent than scientists once believed.

Dogs are smart enough to react to and understand human emotions and body language.

Dogs observe different clues humans give based on their actions. For example, in one common test of dog intelligence, a human hides a treat under one of several upside-down cups. If the human points to the cup with the treat, the dog will understand. It will follow the pointed finger to the cup with the treat underneath.

Dogs also react to human body language. When humans are angry, their postures, movements, and facial expressions show this emotion. A dog will see this look and move away from the human.

Matching Games

Dogs learn to match spoken words with objects in the same way human children do. If a dog is given a new word and a new object, it will begin to understand the new word and object are linked.

Some border collies take this idea to an extreme. One intelligence test studies a border collie's ability to match a picture with a real object. First the border collie is shown a photo of an object, such as a pumpkin. The dog studies the photo of the pumpkin. Then it fetches the actual pumpkin.

Brainy Border Collie

Chaser is a well-trained border collie. She is told the name of a toy and can find the specific toy from a large pile. In one test, Chaser is told to find an octopus toy named Inky. She moves hundreds of colorful stuffed toys and balls searching for Inky. After a few seconds, Chaser finds the green octopus toy. Chaser has an amazing vocabulary. She knows the names of all 1,022 of her toys. That makes this border collie one of the smartest dogs in the world.

Go to the Head of the Class

In the 1990s, dog obedience experts ranked dog breeds based on intelligence. Everyone wanted his or her breed to be considered the smartest. A top rank meant the breed understood new commands, obeyed, and remembered the commands immediately. Breeds at the bottom of the list needed the commands repeated up to 100 times.

The border collie scored the top rank. Other bright breeds were the poodle, the German shepherd, the golden retriever, and the Doberman pinscher. At the bottom of the list were the borzoi, the chow chow, the bulldog,

First Alert

Some dogs can sense Earth-shaking waves before a disaster happens. Dogs have been known to display strange behavior hours and days before an earthquake. They pace and act worried. Scientists believe that dogs' sharp hearing helps them forecast quakes. Dogs may respond to high-frequency sounds that announce an earthquake, such as rocks breaking deep below the earth.

Bloodhounds are great at sniffing out a scent, but they may not be the best at passing an obedience test.

and the basenji. The Afghan hound was ranked at the end.

All dogs have a natural intelligence for which they have been bred. For example a bloodhound might not pass an obedience test, but it would do better at tracking a scent trail to find a missing person.

CHAPTER FOUR

FROM THE WILD TO THE HOUSE

All household dogs descend from the gray wolf. Household dogs share their family tree with 39 wild relatives. All of these carnivorous mammals belong to the Canidae family. Some of these species, such as the wolf, coyote, and fox, make their homes across the United States.

Other wild canids live around the world. They are found on every continent except Antarctica.

The household dog descended from the gray wolf.

Sharp front and back teeth are features that household dogs and wild canids share.

They range from the dingo of Australia to the New Guinea singing dog. The dhole of India, the raccoon dog of China, the African wild dog of South Africa, and the South American bush dog are all wild canids too.

Household dogs and wild canids share some features. Wild canids are medium-sized with long legs for hunting prey over great distances. Their long noses have well-developed jaws. They have front teeth that can shred meat and back teeth that can crush vegetables and bones.

Canidae Communications

Household dogs behave similarly to wild members of the Canidae family. They use body language to communicate. Confident dogs walk on their toes with heads held high. Their ears are up and forward with eyes staring straight. If dogs sense a challenge, confident dogs will curl their upper lips, bare their teeth, and walk stiff legged with an upright tail. Nervous dogs tuck in their tails, keep their ears flat, show their bellies, and avoid eye contact.

Friendly dogs wiggle their rears and sweep their tails with a low wag. Playful dogs bow. They slide their front legs out, raise their hind ends, and excitedly wag their tails.

Household dogs and wild canids also communicate verbally. They whine for attention, bark when they sense danger, and growl when in danger. Even the pitch and pace of barks can express different

Dogs and wild canids have different barks and sounds for special situations.

messages. Dogs give a sharp single bark when they are separated from their families. A lower and harsher series of barks signals that strangers are approaching. Unevenly spaced, high-pitched barks point out that it is playtime.

Caveman's First Pet

Household dogs came from their largest wild relative: the gray wolf. Dogs were the first animals humans made pets. The humans gained protection from other wild animals, and they gained a hunting companion. The dogs earned tasty scraps and a warm spot in front of the fire.

Gradually humans developed separate dog breeds. They carefully chose dogs for certain traits and bred them. Approximately 4,000 years ago, two of the first household dog breeds appeared. Greyhounds were bred to have keen eyesight, so they could race after prey and capture it. Mastiffs were bred for courage and powerful muscles, so they could guard homes and cattle.

Dog Fancy

The first dog show kicked off in England in 1859. This event featured 60 dogs competing against each other in athletic ability. All of the contestants were sporting dogs, either pointers or setters. Hunters acted as judges. Instead of trophies, winners received guns. Sportsmen in the United States started the Westminster Kennel Club in 1877. Their first show also starred sporting dogs. Today most dog shows are based on appearance. Now purebreds from the affenpinscher to the Yorkshire terrier compete for the Best in Show title. This title is given to the winning dog each year.

At one time, a dog pack was a status symbol.

Dogs for Work and Leisure

During the Middle Ages (500–1500 CE) careful breeding increased. The nobility wanted different types of dogs for hunting. Beagles tracked rabbits for human hunting parties. Terriers hunted animals living in underground holes. Retrievers jumped into lakes and used their mouths to fetch ducks. Other dogs, like Norwegian elkhounds and Irish wolfhounds, were named for the prey they hunted.

Around the Renaissance period (1500–1688 CE), miniature breeds, such as the English toy spaniel, became popular with wealthy people. These companion dogs did not serve a purpose other than snuggling in laps. Various breeds continued to be bred for hunting and other work.

Dog Dilemmas

Approximately 78 million dogs are loved as pets today. However other dogs are not as lucky. Each year many companion animals enter animal shelters. These animals could be abandoned dogs, stray dogs, or dogs that have attacked humans. Due to lack of adoptive homes, approximately 60 percent of all dogs in shelters are humanely euthanized.

Modern household dogs face another challenge: overbreeding.

Stopping Pet Overpopulation

Dogs are popular pets, but having too many dogs means some end up in shelters. Humans can reduce the population of homeless pets by having their pets spayed or neutered. These surgeries ensure that dogs cannot produce puppies. In six years, one unspayed female and her offspring could give birth to 67,000 puppies.

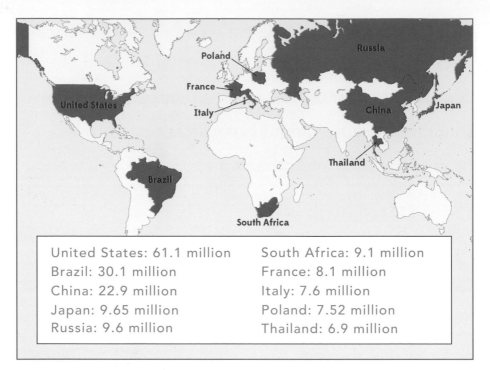

Worldly Dogs

This map shows the ten countries with the highest pet dog populations. The United States has the largest dog population in the world with more than 61 million. The other nine countries shown on this map also have high numbers of dogs. Brazil, at number two, has approximately 30 million dogs. How does this map give you a better understanding of dog populations around the world?

People who breed purebred dogs end up breeding dogs with health problems. Bulldogs are bred for flat faces and huge heads, but they have breathing problems and cannot give birth naturally. Sharpeis get skin infections between their wrinkly folds. Dachshunds suffer from ruptured disks in their long backs. Giant breeds, such as the Saint Bernard, get arthritis in their hips. Miniature breeds, such as Chihuahuas, suffer from heart problems.

Responsible breeders make certain the mother and father dogs are healthy before breeding. These breeders test for genetic diseases. Then they breed for health and behavior.

FURTHER EVIDENCE

There is quite a bit of information in this chapter about how dogs share behaviors with their wild relative, the gray wolf. If you could pick out the main point of the chapter, what would it be? What evidence was given to support that point? Visit the Web site below to learn more about dog behaviors. Choose a quote from the Web site that relates to this chapter. Does this quote support the author's main point? Does it make a new point? Write a few sentences explaining how the quote you found relates to this chapter.

Gray Wolves

www.mycorelibrary.com/dogs

DIFFERENT DOG JOBS

Most dogs already have the important job of being a companion to humans. But many dogs tackle a variety of specific jobs to assist humans.

Therapy dogs visit people in hospitals and nursing homes. These calm dogs lift spirits, help with physical therapy, and boost health. Therapy dogs receive

Dogs have a variety of important jobs that help humans, including being library therapy dogs.

special training so they are comfortable with strangers and different environments.

Service dogs perform tasks that help people with disabilities. They may partner with blind people and guide them. They also partner with deaf people. Dogs can warn these people of household sounds, such as doorbells and fire alarms. Some service dogs can sense when a person is about to have a seizure. This helps the person find a safe spot to lie down before the seizure occurs. Service dogs also help physically disabled people. Trained dogs can pick up dropped items, open doors, turn on lights, and call 911.

Who Let the Dog in the Library?

Libraries around the country are opening their doors to dogs. Specially trained therapy dogs encourage children to read books. They are patient listeners. Readers paired with dogs improve their reading skills along with their self-confidence.

Lifesaving Dogs

Military dogs have served our nation since its earliest days. These dogs guard, patrol, scout, and track.

Seizure alert dogs like Lady are trained to warn an adult when their partners are having a seizure or before they have a seizure.

They save lives by finding explosives, mines, and weapons.

Police dogs also save lives. They perform search and rescue missions to find missing people. They help law enforcement by using their noses to sniff out illegal drugs and explosives.

Some dogs are trained to help police officers keep people safe. They are trained to sniff out drugs and explosives.

Dog Tests

Scientists study dogs searching for new ways to use their intelligence. One experiment proved dogs disobey orders when they are in dark rooms. The tests show dogs understand humans cannot see them misbehaving in the dark. Dogs' ability to think and understand a human's point of view could help us better train them.

Dogs are favorite household pets, as well as smart and helpful companions. These super-smart animals are trained to assist humans in everyday activities. It is important for humans to care for dogs, so these intelligent animals will continue to be human companions for years to come.

EXPLORE ONLINE

The focus in Chapter Five was on dogs that perform different jobs. The Web site below has even more information about dogs that have jobs. As you know, every source is different. How is the information given on the Web site different from the information in this chapter? What information is the same? How do the two sources present information differently? What can you learn from this Web site?

Dogs with Jobs
www.mycorelibrary.com/dogs

Common Name: Dog

Scientific Name: *Canis lupus familiaris*

Average Size: From four inches (10 cm) high (Chihuahua) to three and a half feet (1 m) high (Great Dane)

Average Weight: From 6 pounds (3 kg) (Chihuahua) to 343 pounds (156 kg) (English mastiff)

Color: Varies depending on breed

Average Lifespan: 6 to 12 years

Diet: Primarily omnivores

Habitat: Worldwide, except for Antarctica

Threats: Humans, overbreeding, overpopulation

Intelligence Features

- Dogs solve problems using trial and error or by watching humans.
- Dogs respond to signals and react to body language.
- Dogs can match words with objects, similar to humans.
- Some dogs perform jobs to assist humans, such as being a therapy dog.

You Are There

Chapter Five discusses how service dogs help people with disabilities. Imagine you have a disability. Write 300 words about your experience. How would a specially trained dog help change your life? What tasks could a dog help perform that would increase your independence?

Another View

There are many different sources about dogs. Each source is a little bit different. Ask a librarian or another adult to help you find a reliable source about dogs. Write a short essay comparing and contrasting the new source's point of view to the ideas in this book. How are the sources similar? How are the sources different? Why do you think they are similar or different?

Surprise Me

Learning about dogs can be interesting and surprising. Think about what you learned from this book. Can you name two or three facts in this book that surprised you? Write a short paragraph about each. Describe what you found surprising and why.

Tell the Tale

Chapter Four discusses how wolves eventually became household pets. Write 200 words that tell the story of how early humans and wolves interacted. Be sure to set the scene, develop a sequence of events, and offer a conclusion.

GLOSSARY

American Kennel Club
a registry of purebred dog pedigrees

body language
movements, postures, and facial expressions that express feelings

breed
animals with identifiable characteristics that separate them from other members of that species

carnivorous
flesh eating

color-blind
the inability to recognize one or more colors

disability
limitations with everyday tasks

euthanize
killing with as little pain as possible

genetic
related to or involving genes, or what characteristics a living thing might have

purebred
bred from members of a recognized breed without mixture of another breed over many generations

socialize
to train an animal or human so it interacts appropriately with others

LEARN MORE

Books

American Kennel Club. *The Complete Dog Book.*
New York: Ballantine Books, 2006.

Coren, Stanley. *The Intelligence of Dogs.* New York:
The Free Press, 2005.

Hare, Brian, and Vanessa Woods. *The Genius of
Dogs: How Dogs Are Smarter than You Think.*
New York: Dutton, 2013.

Web Links

To learn more about dogs, visit ABDO Publishing
Company online at **www.abdopublishing.com**. Web
sites about dogs are featured on our Book Links page.
These links are routinely monitored and updated to
provide the most current information available.
Visit **www.mycorelibrary.com** for free additional tools
for teachers and students.

INDEX

ABOUT THE AUTHOR

Nancy Furstinger is the author of nearly 100 books, including many on her favorite topic: animals! Nancy shares her home with her rescued dogs: Lacy, a Labrador retriever, and Bosco, a rottweiler mix.